P9-CLU-332

Light Cooking™

PASTA, BEANS & RICE

Healthy, Low Fat and Delicious!

PUBLICATIONS INTERNATIONAL, LTD.

Copyright © 1995 by Publications International, Ltd.
All rights reserved. This publication may not be reproduced or quoted in whole or in part by mimeograph or any other printed or electronic means, or for presentation on radio, television, videotape or film without written permission from:

Louis Weber, C.E.O.
Publications International, Ltd.
7373 N. Cicero Ave.
Lincolnwood, IL 60646

Permission is never granted for commercial purposes.

Light Cooking is a trademark of Publications International, Ltd.

Food Guide Pyramid source: U.S. Department of Agriculture/U.S. Department of Health and Human Services.

Recipe Development: Nanette Blanchard, Debby Maugans, Mary Jane Laws
Nutritional Analysis: Linda R. Yoakam, M.S., R.D.

Photography: Photo/Kevin Smith, Chicago
Photographers: Kevin Smith, Doug Hunter
Prop Stylist: Wendy Marx
Food Stylists: Tobe LeMoine, Irene Bertolucci, Teri Rys-Maki, Jeff Anthony
Assistant Food Stylists: Corrine Kozlak, Kim Hartman

Pictured on the front cover: Shrimp and Snow Peas with Fusilli *(page 46)*.
Pictured on the inside front cover: Polenta with Black Bean Salsa *(page 90)*.
Pictured on the inside back cover: Thai Chicken Broccoli Salad *(page 28)*.
Pictured on the back cover *(top to bottom):* Cheese Ravioli with Pumpkin Sauce *(page 62)*, Southwestern Bean and Corn Salad *(page 30)*, Beef & Bean Burritos *(page 44)* and White Chili Pilaf *(page 68)*.

ISBN: 0-7853-1198-X

Manufactured in U.S.A.

8 7 6 5 4 3 2 1

CONTENTS

LESSONS IN SMART EATING

Today, people everywhere are more aware than ever before about the importance of maintaining a healthful lifestyle. In addition to proper exercise, this includes eating foods that are lower in fat, sodium and cholesterol. The goal of *Light Cooking* is to provide today's cook with easy-to-prepare recipes that taste great, yet easily fit into your dietary goals. Eating well is a matter of making smarter choices about the foods you eat. Preparing the recipes in *Light Cooking* is your first step toward making smart choices a delicious reality.

A Balanced Diet

The U.S. Department of Agriculture and the Department of Health and Human Services have developed a Food Guide Pyramid to illustrate how easy it is to eat a healthier diet. It is not a rigid prescription, but rather a general guide that lets you choose a healthful diet that's right for you. It calls for eating a wide variety of foods to get the nutrients you need and, at the same time, the right amount of calories to maintain a healthy weight.

Food Guide Pyramid
A Guide to Daily Food Choices

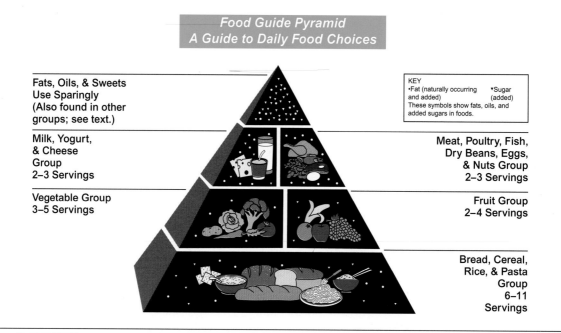

Fats, Oils, & Sweets
Use Sparingly
(Also found in other groups; see text.)

KEY
•Fat (naturally occurring and added)   ▼Sugar (added)
These symbols show fats, oils, and added sugars in foods.

Milk, Yogurt, & Cheese Group
2–3 Servings

Meat, Poultry, Fish, Dry Beans, Eggs, & Nuts Group
2–3 Servings

Vegetable Group
3–5 Servings

Fruit Group
2–4 Servings

Bread, Cereal, Rice, & Pasta Group
6–11 Servings

The number of servings, and consequently, the number of calories a person can eat each day, is determined by a number of factors, including age, weight, height, activity level and gender. Sedentary women and some older adults need about 1,600 calories each day. For most children, teenage girls, active women and many sedentary men 2,000 calories is about right. Teenage boys, active men and some very active women use about 2,800 calories each day. Use the chart below to determine how many servings you need for your calorie level.

Personalized Food Group Servings for Different Calorie Levels*			
	1,600	2,000	2,800
Bread Group Servings	6	8	11
Vegetable Group Servings	3	4	5
Fruit Group Servings	2	3	4
Milk Group Servings	2-3**	2-3**	2-3**
Meat Group Servings (ounces)	5	6	7

* Numbers may be rounded.
** Women who are pregnant or breast-feeding, teenagers and young adults to age 24 need 3 or more servings.

Lower Fat for Healthier Living

It is widely known that most Americans' diets are too high in fat. A low fat diet reduces your risk of getting certain diseases and helps you maintain a healthy weight. Studies have shown that eating more than the recommended amount of fat (especially saturated fat) is associated with increased blood cholesterol levels in some adults. A high blood cholesterol level is associated with increased risk for heart disease. A high fat diet may also increase your chances for obesity and some types of cancer.

Nutrition experts recommend diets that contain 30% or less of total daily calories from fat. The "30% calories from fat" goal applies to a total diet over time, not to a single food, serving of a recipe or meal. To find the approximate percentage of calories from fat use this easy 3-step process:

1 Multiply the grams of fat per serving by 9 (there are 9 calories in each gram of fat) to give you the number of calories from fat per serving.

2 Divide by the total number of calories per serving.

3 Multiply by 100%.

For example, imagine a 200 calorie sandwich that has 10 grams of fat.
To find the percentage of calories from fat, first multiply the grams of fat by 9: $10 \times 9 = 90$

Then, divide by the total number of calories in a serving:
$$90 \div 200 = .45$$

Multiply by 100% to get the percentage of calories from fat:
$$.45 \times 100\% = 45\%$$

You may find doing all this math tiresome, so an easier way to keep track of the fat in your diet is to calculate the total *grams* of fat appropriate to your caloric intake, then keep a running count of fat grams over the course of a day. The Nutrition Reference Chart on page 92 lists recommended daily fat intakes based on calorie level.

Defining "Fat Free"

It is important to take the time to read food labels carefully. For example, you'll find many food products on the grocery store shelves making claims such as "97% fat free." This does not necessarily mean that 97% of the *calories* are free from fat (or that only 3 percent of calories come from fat). Often these numbers are calculated by weight. This means that out of 100 grams of this food, 3 grams are fat. Depending on what else is in the food, the percentage of calories from fat can be quite high. You may find that the percent of calories *from fat* can be as high as 50%.

Daily Values

Fat has become the focus of many diets and eating plans. This is because most Americans' diets are too high in fat. However, there are other important nutrients to be aware of including saturated fat, sodium, cholesterol, protein, carbohydrates and several vitamins and minerals. Daily values for these nutrients have been established by the government and reflect current nutritional recommendations for a 2,000 calorie reference diet. They are appropriate for most adults and children (age 4 or older) and provide excellent guidelines for an overall healthy diet. The chart on page 92 gives the daily values for the nutrients listed in this publication.

Nutritional Analysis

Every recipe in *Light Cooking* is followed by a nutritional analysis block that lists certain nutrient values for a single serving.

■   The analysis of each recipe includes all the ingredients that are listed in that recipe, *except* ingredients labeled as "optional" or for "garnish."

■   If a range is offered for an ingredient ("¼ to ⅛ teaspoon" for example), the *first* amount given was used to calculate the nutrition information.

■ If an ingredient is presented with an option ("2 cups hot cooked rice or noodles" for example), the *first* item listed was used to calculate the nutrition information.

■ Foods shown in photographs on the same serving plate and offered as "serve with" suggestions at the end of a recipe are *not* included in the recipe analysis unless they are listed in the ingredient list.

■ In recipes calling for cooked rice or noodles, the analysis was based on rice or noodles that were prepared without added salt or fat unless otherwise mentioned in the recipe.

The nutrition information that appears with each recipe was calculated by an independent nutrition consulting firm. Every effort has been made to check the accuracy of these numbers. However, because numerous variables account for a wide range of values in certain foods, all analyses that appear in this book should be considered approximate.

The recipes in this publication are *not* intended as a medically therapeutic program, nor as a substitute for medically approved diet plans for people on fat, cholesterol or sodium restricted diets. You should consult your physician before beginning any diet plan. The recipes offered here can be a part of a healthy lifestyle that meets recognized dietary guidelines. A healthy lifestyle includes not only eating a balanced diet, but engaging in proper exercise as well.

All the ingredients called for in these recipes are generally available in large supermarkets, so there is no need to go to specialty or health food stores. You'll also see an ever-increasing amount of reduced fat and nonfat products available in local markets. Take advantage of these items to reduce your daily fat intake even more.

Cooking Healthier

When cooking great-tasting low fat meals, you will find some techniques or ingredients are different from traditional cooking. Fat serves as a flavor enhancer and gives foods a distinctive and desirable texture. In order to compensate for the lack of fat and still get great-tasting results, many of the *Light Cooking* recipes call for a selection of herbs or a combination of fresh vegetables. Often meat is included in a recipe as an accent flavor rather than the star attraction. Vegetables are often "sautéed" in a small amount of broth rather than oil. These are all simple changes that you can easily make when you start cooking healthy!

Pasta Basics

Pasta, which translates as paste in Italian, comes from one of two starchy doughs—one made with eggs, one without. Egg doughs made with all-purpose flour and eggs are preferred by home cooks because they are easy to roll out and cut by hand. Eggless doughs made with semolina flour and water are more suited for commercially prepared pasta because semolina flour produces a dough that withstands mass production. Both types provide an excellent source of low fat, complex carbohydrates and a good supply of iron, magnesium, thiamin, niacin and riboflavin, making any pasta a perfect choice for healthful eating.

For best results when cooking pasta, follow the package instructions. Oil and salt are often added to the cooking water for flavor and to prevent the water from boiling over. However, they can be omitted without altering the final product, thus reducing added fat and salt in your diet. When cooking pasta, begin checking for doneness after 5 minutes. Pasta is finished cooking when it is tender but still firm to the bite, or al dente. Rinse pasta under cold running water when it is used in chilled salads or in those recipes that require additional handling of it, such as lasagna and stuffed shells. This stops the cooking process and prevents the pasta from sticking together.

Dried, commercially prepared pasta can be stored indefinitely in an airtight container at room temperature. Store fresh or homemade pasta in an airtight container for up to five days in the refrigerator or for up to eight months in the freezer. Do not thaw frozen pasta; cook it directly from the freezer.

Guide to Cooking Pasta				
Dried Pasta	Amount	Water	Boiling Time	Yield
Angel Hair	4 ounces	4 quarts	5-7 minutes	2 cups
Bow Ties	2 cups	4 quarts	10 minutes	2½ cups
Elbow Macaroni	2 cups	4 quarts	10 minutes	3 cups
Fettuccine	4 ounces	4 quarts	8-10 minutes	2 cups
Orzo	2 cups	4 quarts	5-8 minutes	4 cups
Spaghetti	4 ounces	4 quarts	10-12 minutes	2 cups

Bean Basics

Legumes, which include dried beans, peas and lentils, are a nutritional windfall. They provide a low fat, low sodium, cholesterol-free source of protein, are high in complex carbohydrates and fiber and are loaded with many vitamins and minerals, including iron and calcium. Canned beans, also rich in these nutrients, contain a substantial amount of sodium due to processing. Rinsing canned beans under cold running water for 1 minute can eliminate up to 40 percent of added sodium.

Always rinse and sort through legumes before cooking them, discarding any that are shriveled, discolored or cracked. After sorting, most beans are soaked in cold water for at least 6 hours prior to cooking. This reduces the cooking time, softens the beans and removes undigestible sugars that may cause flatulence. Black-eyed peas, lentils and split peas do not need to be soaked before they are cooked. For best results when cooking beans, follow the package instructions and begin checking for doneness at the minimum cooking time. To test for doneness, gently squeeze several beans. When they are tender, remove them from the heat and immediately drain in a colander. If left in their cooking water, beans continue to cook, will lose their shape and may become mushy.

Store dried beans in an airtight container at room temperature for up to one year or in the freezer indefinitely. Place cooked beans in an airtight container and store for up to one week in the refrigerator or freeze for up to six months.

Guide To Cooking Dried Beans				
Dried Bean	Amount	Water	Simmering Time	Yield
Black Beans	1 cup	4 cups	2 hours	2 cups
Black-Eyed Peas	1 cup	8 cups	45 minutes	2½ cups
Garbanzo Beans	1 cup	4 cups	3 hours	2½ cups
Great Northern Beans	1 cup	3½ cups	2 hours	2 cups
Kidney Beans	1 cup	3 cups	45 minutes	2¼ cups
Lentils & Split Peas	1 cup	3 cups	45 minutes	2¼ cups
Pinto Beans	1 cup	3 cups	2½ hours	2 cups

Rice and Grain Basics

Cereal grains, such as wild rice, bulgur and cornmeal, have been food staples for thousands of years because they offer an inexpensive source of low fat protein. While they are often associated with a particular region of the world—rice with Asia and cornmeal with the southern United States and Italy—many star in a variety of cuisines worldwide.

Rice is a staple for more than half the world's population making it one of the most popular grains. It is classified according to the length of its grains. Long grain is the most common type of rice and is interchangeable with medium grain rice. Short grain rice contains more starch than long and medium grains. This makes the grains very sticky when cooked. Wild rice, which has a chewy texture and earthy flavor, is often classified as a rice, yet it is actually the seed of an aquatic marsh grass native to Minnesota.

Most packages of grains come with specific directions for cooking. For best results, always follow the package directions. Although oil and salt are often added during the cooking of some grains to increase flavor, they can be omitted without significantly altering the final product. Simmer all rice until it is tender but still firm to the bite. Bulgur should be simmered until tender and fluffy; cornmeal until tender but pourable.

Store all uncooked grains in airtight containers. White rice and wild rice can be stored at room temperature indefinitely; brown rice for up to six months. Store all cooked rice in an airtight container for up to one week in the refrigerator or for up to six months in the freezer. Store uncooked bulgur in an airtight container for up to one year at room temperature or two years in the freezer; cornmeal for up to one month in the refrigerator or for up to two years in the freezer. Store cooked bulgur and cornmeal in airtight containers for up to one week in the refrigerator or for up to six months in the freezer.

Guide To Cooking Grains & Rice				
Grain	Amount	Water	Simmering Time	Yield
Arborio Rice	1 cup	1½ cups	20 minutes	2 cups
Basmati Rice	1 cup	2½ cups	20 minutes	3 cups
Brown Rice	1 cup	2 cups	45 minutes	3 cups
Bulgur	1 cup	2 cups	15-20 minutes	2½ cups
Cornmeal	1 cup	2¾ cups	10 minutes	3½ cups
White Rice	1 cup	2 cups	20 minutes	3 cups
Wild Rice	1 cup	2 cups	50 minutes	2⅔ cups

Pasta, Bean and Rice Varieties

1. Orzo Pasta
2. White Basmati Rice
3. Instant White Rice
4. Arborio Rice
5. Wild Rice
6. Black Beans
7. Split Peas
8. Bulgur
9. Couscous
10. Cornmeal (Polenta)

11. Black-Eyed Peas
12. Garbanzo Beans
13. Lima Beans
14. Pinto Beans
15. Cannellini Beans
16. Great Northern Beans
17. Lentils
18. Red Kidney Beans
19. Elbow Macaroni
20. Rotini

21. Angel Hair Pasta
22. Ditalini
23. Bow Tie Pasta
24. Ravioli
25. Radiatore
26. Linguine
27. Spinach Fettuccine
28. Fusilli
29. Small Shell Pasta
30. Lasagna Noodles

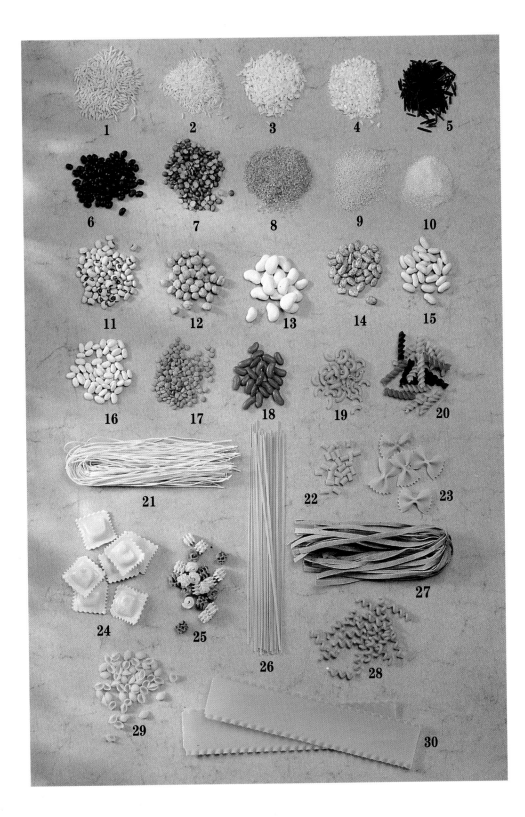

APPETIZERS

MEXICAN ROLL-UPS

Enjoy guacamole the low fat way—rolled up with chunky salsa and nonfat cheese in tasty lasagna noodles. Substituting lasagna noodles for tortilla chips eliminates more than 30% of calories from fat per serving.

6 uncooked lasagna noodles
¾ cup prepared guacamole
¾ cup chunky salsa
¾ cup (3 ounces) shredded nonfat Cheddar cheese

1 Cook lasagna noodles according to package directions, omitting salt. Rinse with cool water; drain. Cool.

2 Layer 2 tablespoons guacamole, 2 tablespoons salsa and 2 tablespoons cheese over each noodle.

3 Roll up noodles jelly-roll fashion. Cut each roll-up in half to form two equal-size roll-ups. Serve immediately with additional salsa, if desired. Or, cover with plastic wrap and refrigerate up to 3 hours before serving. Garnish with peppers, if desired.

Makes 12 appetizers

Nutrients per Serving:

Calories	40
(28% of calories from fat)	
Total Fat	1 g
Saturated Fat	0 g
Cholesterol	2 mg
Sodium	218 mg
Carbohydrate	4 g
Dietary Fiber	1 g
Protein	3 g
Calcium	65 mg
Iron	<1 mg
Vitamin A	35 RE
Vitamin C	5 mg

DIETARY EXCHANGES:
½ Starch/Bread

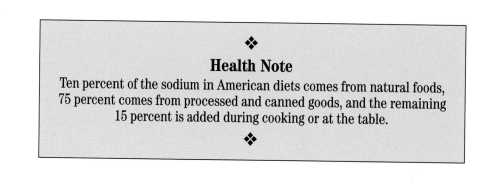

Health Note

Ten percent of the sodium in American diets comes from natural foods, 75 percent comes from processed and canned goods, and the remaining 15 percent is added during cooking or at the table.

VEGETABLE-TOPPED HUMMUS

❖

Look for tahini, a thick paste made from ground sesame seeds, in the ethnic section of major supermarkets, Middle Eastern markets or health food stores.

❖

1 can (about 15 ounces) garbanzo beans (chick-peas), rinsed and drained
2 tablespoons tahini
2 tablespoons lemon juice
1 clove garlic
¾ teaspoon salt
1 tomato, finely chopped
2 green onions, chopped
2 tablespoons chopped fresh parsley

1 Combine garbanzo beans, tahini, lemon juice, garlic and salt in food processor or blender; process until smooth.

2 Combine tomato, onions and parsley in small bowl.

3 Spoon bean mixture into medium serving bowl; spoon tomato mixture evenly over top. Serve with wedges of pita bread or assorted crackers, if desired.

Makes 8 servings

Nutrients per Serving:	
Calories	82
(31% of calories from fat)	
Total Fat	3 g
Saturated Fat	<1 g
Cholesterol	0 mg
Sodium	429 mg
Carbohydrate	11 g
Dietary Fiber	3 g
Protein	3 g
Calcium	32 mg
Iron	2 mg
Vitamin A	22 RE
Vitamin C	10 mg

DIETARY EXCHANGES:
½ Starch/Bread, 1
Vegetable, ½ Fat

❖
Health Note
Diets high in dietary calcium may actually prevent—not promote— the formation of kidney stones. Studies indicate that calcium, abundant in foods like milk, yogurt, cottage cheese and ricotta cheese, appears to bind oxalates that are linked to the formation of the stones.
❖

THAI LAMB & COUSCOUS ROLLS

❖

Nutrient-dense cabbage leaves surround a mouthwatering blend of Thai-inspired ingredients.

❖

Nutrients per Serving:

Calories	53
(16% of calories from fat)	
Total Fat	1 g
Saturated Fat	<1 g
Cholesterol	7 mg
Sodium	75 mg
Carbohydrate	7 g
Dietary Fiber	1 g
Protein	4 g
Calcium	34 mg
Iron	<1 mg
Vitamin A	24 RE
Vitamin C	4 mg

DIETARY EXCHANGES:
½ Starch/Bread, ½ Lean Meat

16 large napa or Chinese cabbage leaves, stems trimmed
2 tablespoons minced fresh ginger
1 teaspoon crushed red pepper
⅔ cup uncooked quick-cooking couscous
½ pound ground lean lamb
½ cup chopped green onions
3 cloves garlic, minced
¼ cup plus 2 tablespoons minced fresh cilantro or mint, divided
2 tablespoons reduced sodium soy sauce
1 tablespoon lime juice
1 teaspoon Oriental sesame oil
1 cup plain nonfat yogurt

1 Place 4 cups water in medium saucepan; bring to a boil over high heat. Drop cabbage leaves into water; cook 30 seconds. Drain in colander. Rinse leaves under cold water until cool; pat dry with paper towels.

2 Place 1 cup water, ginger and pepper in medium saucepan; bring to a boil over high heat. Stir in couscous; cover. Remove saucepan from heat; let stand 5 minutes.

3 Spray large saucepan with nonstick cooking spray; add lamb, onions and garlic. Cook and stir over medium-high heat 5 minutes or until lamb is no longer pink. Remove lamb from skillet; drain in colander.

4 Combine couscous, lamb mixture, ¼ cup cilantro, soy sauce, lime juice and oil in medium bowl; blend well. Spoon evenly down centers of cabbage leaves. Fold ends of cabbage leaves over filling; roll up.

5 Combine yogurt and remaining 2 tablespoons cilantro in small bowl; spoon evenly over rolls. Serve warm. Garnish with red onion slices and edible flowers, if desired.

Makes 16 appetizers

ROASTED VEGETABLE PIZZA

❖

A delightful medley of roasted vegetables and garlic tops this unusual yet delicately flavored pizza crust, making each serving a slice of perfection.

❖

1 cup uncooked white rice
Olive oil flavored nonstick cooking spray
½ cup grated Parmesan cheese
2 egg whites, lightly beaten
1 pound eggplant, peeled and diced
1 large red or purple onion, thinly sliced
1 large red bell pepper, cut into 1-inch pieces
2 tablespoons Italian seasoning
1 can (6 ounces) no-salt-added tomato paste
2 tablespoons balsamic vinegar
¼ teaspoon garlic salt
1 cup (4 ounces) shredded part-skim mozzarella cheese
⅓ cup grated Parmesan cheese

1 Place 2 cups water in medium saucepan; bring to a boil over high heat. Stir in rice. Cover; reduce heat to low. Simmer 20 minutes or until liquid is absorbed and rice is tender. Cool completely.

2 Preheat oven to 450°F. Spray 12-inch nonstick pizza pan and 15×10-inch jelly-roll pan with cooking spray.

3 Combine ½ cup Parmesan cheese and rice in saucepan. Stir in egg whites until well blended. Press rice mixture firmly onto bottom of prepared pizza pan; set aside.

4 Place eggplant, onion and pepper in large resealable plastic food storage bag. Generously spray with cooking spray; add Italian seasoning. Seal bag; turn to coat. Place vegetables in prepared jelly-roll pan. Bake 30 minutes or until vegetables are tender, stirring after 15 minutes. Remove vegetables from oven.

5 *Reduce oven temperature to 400°F.* Combine tomato paste, vinegar and garlic salt in large bowl. Add roasted vegetables; toss to coat. Spoon vegetables evenly onto prepared crust.

6 Bake pizza 10 minutes; top with mozzarella and remaining ⅓ cup Parmesan cheese. Bake 8 minutes or until cheeses are lightly browned. Garnish with sprigs of fresh thyme, if desired.

Makes 12 appetizers

Nutrients per Serving:

Calories	147
(24% of calories from fat)	
Total Fat	4 g
Saturated Fat	2 g
Cholesterol	11 mg
Sodium	237 mg
Carbohydrate	20 g
Dietary Fiber	2 g
Protein	8 g
Calcium	185 mg
Iron	2 mg
Vitamin A	78 RE
Vitamin C	13 mg

DIETARY EXCHANGES:
1 Starch/Bread, 1 Lean Meat, 1 Vegetable

PASTA E FAGIOLI

❖

White beans and pasta shells combine in this traditional Italian soup. White beans, which are loaded with soluble fiber, help reduce total blood cholesterol levels by lowering LDL (bad) cholesterol levels.

❖

2 tablespoons olive oil
1 cup chopped onion
3 cloves garlic, minced
2 cans (14½ ounces each) Italian-style stewed tomatoes, undrained
3 cups ⅓-less-salt chicken broth
1 can (about 15 ounces) cannellini beans (white kidney beans), undrained*
¼ cup chopped fresh Italian parsley
1 teaspoon dried basil leaves
¼ teaspoon ground black pepper
4 ounces uncooked small shell pasta

1 Heat oil in 4-quart Dutch oven over medium-high heat until hot; add onion and garlic. Cook and stir 5 minutes or until onion is tender.

2 Add tomatoes with liquid, chicken broth, beans with liquid, parsley, basil and pepper to Dutch oven; bring to a boil over high heat, stirring occasionally. Reduce heat to low; cover. Simmer 10 minutes.

3 Add pasta to Dutch oven; cover. Simmer 10 to 12 minutes or until pasta is just tender, stirring occasionally. Serve immediately. Serve each serving with wedge of toasted bread, if desired. *Makes 8 servings*

*One can (about 15 ounces) Great Northern beans, undrained, may be substituted for cannellini beans.

Nutrients per Serving:	
Calories	217
(23% of calories from fat)	
Total Fat	6 g
Saturated Fat	1 g
Cholesterol	0 mg
Sodium	661 mg
Carbohydrate	37 g
Dietary Fiber	6 g
Protein	12 g
Calcium	65 mg
Iron	2 mg
Vitamin A	93 RE
Vitamin C	24 mg

DIETARY EXCHANGES:
2 Starch/Bread, 1
Vegetable, 1 Fat

HOT BLACK BEAN DIP

❖

This spicy bean dip gets its smoky flavor from the chipotle chili pepper. Chipotles, smoke-dried jalapeño peppers, are available dried or canned in adobe sauce. Look for them in the imported section of major supermarkets, Latin American markets or specialty stores.

❖

1 can (about 15 ounces) black beans, rinsed and drained
1 can (about 16 ounces) whole tomatoes, drained and chopped
1 canned chipotle chili in adobe sauce, drained and finely chopped*
1 teaspoon dried oregano leaves
1 cup (4 ounces) shredded reduced fat Cheddar cheese

1 Place beans in medium bowl; mash with fork or potato masher until smooth.

2 Place beans in heavy, small saucepan. Add tomatoes, chipotle chili and oregano; blend well. Cook over medium heat 5 minutes or until heated through, stirring occasionally.

3 Remove saucepan from heat. Add cheese; stir constantly until cheese melts.

4 Spoon bean dip into serving bowl. Garnish with fresh vegetables. Serve hot with tortilla chips, if desired. *Makes 8 servings*

*Chipotle chilies can sting and irritate the skin; wear rubber gloves when handling chilies and do not touch eyes.

Nutrients per Serving:

Calories	92
(22% of calories from fat)	
Total Fat	3 g
Saturated Fat	1 g
Cholesterol	8 mg
Sodium	458 mg
Carbohydrate	13 g
Dietary Fiber	4 g
Protein	8 g
Calcium	121 mg
Iron	1 mg
Vitamin A	114 RE
Vitamin C	9 mg

DIETARY EXCHANGES:
½ Starch/Bread, 1 Vegetable, ½ Fat

❖

Cook's Tip
When exposed to high temperatures during cooking, cheese may turn stringy, rubbery or grainy. Avoid this problem by adding the cheese toward the end of the cooking process and cooking over low heat just until the cheese melts.

❖

VEGETABLE & COUSCOUS FILLED TOMATOES

❖

Good-for-you garlic teams up with couscous in these crowd-pleasing appetizers. New research has linked the consumption of at least 1 clove of garlic a day to reduced rates of stomach cancer, leading many to believe that a clove a day may help keep the doctor away.

❖

Nutrients per Serving:

Calories	65
(14% of calories from fat)	
Total Fat	1 g
Saturated Fat	<1 g
Cholesterol	0 mg
Sodium	20 mg
Carbohydrate	13 g
Dietary Fiber	3 g
Protein	2 g
Calcium	20 mg
Iron	1 mg
Vitamin A	86 RE
Vitamin C	29 mg

DIETARY EXCHANGES:
½ Starch/Bread, 1½ Vegetable

½ cup ⅓-less-salt chicken broth
2 teaspoons olive oil
⅓ cup uncooked quick-cooking couscous
18 large plum tomatoes
   Nonstick cooking spray
1 cup diced zucchini
⅓ cup sliced green onions
2 cloves garlic, minced
2 tablespoons chopped fresh Italian parsley
1½ teaspoons Dijon mustard
½ teaspoon Italian seasoning

1 Combine chicken broth and oil in small saucepan; bring to a boil over high heat. Stir in couscous; cover. Remove saucepan from heat; let stand 5 minutes or until couscous is tender.

2 Cut thin slice from top of each tomato; discard slices. Remove pulp from tomatoes, leaving ⅛-inch-thick shells; reserve pulp. Place tomatoes cut side down on paper towels to drain. Meanwhile, drain excess liquid from reserved pulp; chop pulp to measure ⅔ cup.

3 Spray large nonstick skillet with cooking spray; heat over medium heat until hot. Add zucchini, onions and garlic. Cook and stir 5 minutes or until vegetables are tender.

4 Combine couscous, reserved ⅔ cup tomato pulp, zucchini mixture, parsley, mustard and Italian seasoning in large bowl; blend well. Spoon couscous mixture evenly into tomato shells. Garnish with decorative lime peels, if desired. *Makes 18 appetizers*

SALADS

THAI CHICKEN BROCCOLI SALAD

❖

Protein-packed white rice is a wonderful substitute for linguine.

❖

4 ounces uncooked linguine
  Nonstick cooking spray
½ pound boneless skinless chicken breasts, cut into 2×½-inch pieces
2 cups broccoli flowerets
⅔ cup chopped red bell pepper
6 green onions, sliced diagonally into 1-inch pieces
¼ cup reduced fat creamy peanut butter
2 tablespoons reduced sodium soy sauce
2 teaspoons Oriental sesame oil
½ teaspoon crushed red pepper
⅛ teaspoon garlic powder
¼ cup unsalted peanuts, chopped

1 Cook pasta according to package directions, omitting salt. Drain; keep warm.

2 Spray large nonstick skillet with cooking spray; heat over medium-high heat until hot. Add chicken; stir-fry 5 minutes or until chicken is no longer pink. Remove chicken from skillet; keep warm.

3 Add broccoli and 2 tablespoons cold water to skillet; cover. Cook 2 minutes. Uncover; cook and stir 2 minutes or until broccoli is crisp-tender. Remove broccoli from skillet. Combine pasta, chicken, broccoli, bell pepper and onions in large bowl.

4 Combine peanut butter, 2 tablespoons hot water, soy sauce, oil, red pepper and garlic powder in small bowl until well blended. Drizzle over pasta mixture; toss to coat. Top each serving evenly with peanuts. Garnish with fresh herbs and carrot strips, if desired.

Makes 4 servings

Nutrients per Serving:

Calories	275
(29% of calories from fat)	
Total Fat	9 g
Saturated Fat	2 g
Cholesterol	29 mg
Sodium	314 mg
Carbohydrate	29 g
Dietary Fiber	4 g
Protein	20 g
Calcium	41 mg
Iron	2 mg
Vitamin A	145 RE
Vitamin C	78 mg

DIETARY EXCHANGES:
1½ Starch/Bread, 2 Lean Meat, 1 Vegetable, ½ Fat

SOUTHWESTERN BEAN AND CORN SALAD

This outstanding salad is dressed with a mixture of vinegar and honey that mellows the heat supplied by mustard, cumin and cayenne pepper.

1 can (about 15 ounces) pinto beans, rinsed and drained
1 cup fresh (about 2 ears) or thawed frozen whole kernel corn
1 red bell pepper, finely chopped
4 green onions, finely chopped
2 tablespoons cider vinegar
2 tablespoons honey
½ teaspoon salt
½ teaspoon ground mustard
½ teaspoon ground cumin
⅛ teaspoon cayenne pepper

1 Combine beans, corn, bell pepper and onions in large bowl.

2 Blend vinegar and honey in small bowl until smooth. Stir in salt, mustard, cumin and cayenne pepper; blend well. Drizzle over bean mixture; toss to coat. Cover; refrigerate 2 hours before serving. Serve on lettuce leaves, if desired.

Makes 4 servings

Nutrients per Serving:

Calories	163
(3% of calories from fat)	
Total Fat	1 g
Saturated Fat	<1 g
Cholesterol	0 mg
Sodium	608 mg
Carbohydrate	36 g
Dietary Fiber	1 g
Protein	7 g
Calcium	54 mg
Iron	2 mg
Vitamin A	50 RE
Vitamin C	21 mg

DIETARY EXCHANGES: 2 Starch/Bread, 1 Vegetable

Cook's Tip

Canned beans are high in sodium. However, researchers have found that rinsing canned beans under running water for 1 minute eliminates up to 40 percent of the sodium.

MEDITERRANEAN PASTA SALAD

Today's health-conscious cooks are increasing their appetite for Mediterranean cuisine. Mediterranean meals, rich in whole grains, fruits, vegetables and legumes, have been linked to a reduced risk of developing heart disease and certain cancers.

2 ounces uncooked bow tie pasta
1 cup rinsed, drained canned garbanzo beans (chick-peas)
1 cup cooked canned artichoke hearts, rinsed, drained, quartered
¾ cup sliced zucchini, halved
¼ cup chopped red onion
3 tablespoons lemon juice
2 tablespoons olive oil
½ teaspoon Italian seasoning
⅛ teaspoon ground black pepper
⅛ teaspoon garlic powder
2 tablespoons crumbled feta cheese

1 Cook pasta according to package directions, omitting salt. Rinse with cool water; drain. Cool.

2 Combine pasta, beans, artichoke hearts, zucchini and onion in large bowl.

3 Blend lemon juice, oil, Italian seasoning, pepper and garlic powder in small bowl until smooth.

4 Drizzle lemon juice mixture over pasta mixture; toss to coat. Top each serving evenly with cheese. Serve on lettuce leaves, if desired. Garnish with Italian parsley, if desired.

Makes 6 servings

Nutrients per Serving:

Calories	101
(27% of calories from fat)	
Total Fat	3 g
Saturated Fat	<1 g
Cholesterol	0 mg
Sodium	142 mg
Carbohydrate	16 g
Dietary Fiber	3 g
Protein	4 g
Calcium	32 mg
Iron	2 mg
Vitamin A	14 RE
Vitamin C	10 mg

DIETARY EXCHANGES:
½ Starch/Bread, 2 Vegetable, ½ Fat

Health Note
Maintaining weight loss is one of the hardest obstacles of dieting. To help preserve your new figure, try desinging a healthful eating plan that includes whole grains, fruits, vegetables, lean meats and low fat dairy products, and increasing your level of physical activity.

FAR EAST TABBOULEH

❖

This refreshing salad is the perfect accompaniment to today's lighter meals.

❖

Nutrients per Serving:

Calories	73
(23% of calories from fat)	
Total Fat	2 g
Saturated Fat	<1 g
Cholesterol	0 mg
Sodium	156 mg
Carbohydrate	13 g
Dietary Fiber	3 g
Protein	2 g
Calcium	16 mg
Iron	1 mg
Vitamin A	51 RE
Vitamin C	9 mg

DIETARY EXCHANGES:
½ Starch/Bread,
1 Vegetable

¾ cup uncooked bulgur
2 tablespoons reduced sodium teriyaki sauce
2 tablespoons lemon juice
1 tablespoon olive oil
¾ cup diced seeded cucumber
¾ cup diced seeded tomato
½ cup thinly sliced green onions
½ cup chopped fresh cilantro or parsley
1 tablespoon minced fresh ginger
1 clove garlic, minced

1 Combine bulgur and 1¾ cups boiling water in small bowl. Cover with plastic wrap; let stand 45 minutes or until bulgur is puffed, stirring occasionally. Drain in wire mesh sieve; discard liquid.

2 Combine bulgur, teriyaki sauce, lemon juice and oil in large bowl. Stir in cucumber, tomato, onions, cilantro, ginger and garlic until well blended. Cover; refrigerate 4 hours before serving, stirring occasionally. Serve over fresh greens, if desired. Garnish with cucumber rings, tomato wedge and fresh herbs, if desired. *Makes 4 servings*

❖

Health Note

When it comes to reducing the total fat in your diet, it is often the small changes that have the greatest effect. For instance, substituting 1 ounce of pretzels for 1 ounce of potato chips eliminates more than 9 grams of fat.

❖

HOPPIN' JOHN SALAD

❖

Many believe that black-eyed peas, also called cowpeas, bring good luck when served on New Year's Day.

❖

Nutrients per Serving:

Calories	242
(16% of calories from fat)	
Total Fat	4 g
Saturated Fat	1 g
Cholesterol	7 mg
Sodium	376 mg
Carbohydrate	39 g
Dietary Fiber	8 g
Protein	12 g
Calcium	40 mg
Iron	2 mg
Vitamin A	54 RE
Vitamin C	6 mg

DIETARY EXCHANGES:
2½ Starch/Bread, ½ Lean Meat, ½ Vegetable, ½ Fat

3 cups dried black-eyed peas, rinsed and drained*
3 cups cooked white rice
¼ pound cooked Canadian bacon, chopped
1 small red onion, chopped
1 rib celery, thinly sliced
2 tablespoons red wine vinegar
1 tablespoon vegetable oil
1 clove garlic, minced
1 teaspoon hot pepper sauce
½ teaspoon salt

1 Place 3 quarts water and black-eyed peas in large saucepan; bring to a boil over high heat. Cover; reduce heat to medium-low. Simmer 1 hour or until peas are tender. Rinse with cool water; drain. Cool.

2 Combine peas, rice, bacon, onion and celery in large bowl. Combine vinegar, oil, garlic, hot sauce and salt in small bowl until well blended. Drizzle over pea mixture; toss to coat. Cover; refrigerate 2 hours before serving. Serve in corn husks, if desired. Garnish with strips of zucchini and pepper slices, if desired. *Makes 6 servings*

*Packages of dried beans may contain grit and tiny stones. Therefore, thoroughly rinse beans. Then sort through and discard grit or any unusual looking pieces.

❖

Health Note
Canola oil has the lowest percentage of saturated fat of any vegetable oil. Saturated fat, which interferes with the removal of fat and cholesterol from the body, should comprise only 10 percent of total calories (approximately 20 g for a 2,000 calorie diet).

❖

ZESTY PASTA SALAD

Lively Italian salad dressing adds zip to this tasty salad.

3 ounces uncooked tri-color rotini pasta
1 cup sliced mushrooms
¾ cup undrained pasta-ready canned tomatoes
½ cup sliced green bell pepper
¼ cup chopped onion
¼ cup fat free Italian salad dressing
2 tablespoons grated Parmesan cheese

1 Cook pasta according to package directions, omitting salt. Rinse with cool water; drain. Cool.

2 Combine pasta, mushrooms, tomatoes with liquid, pepper and onion in large bowl. Pour Italian dressing over pasta mixture; toss to coat.

3 Serve on lettuce leaves, if desired. Top each serving evenly with cheese.

Makes 6 servings

Nutrients per Serving:

Calories	80
(19% of calories from fat)	
Total Fat	2 g
Saturated Fat	<1 g
Cholesterol	2 mg
Sodium	239 mg
Carbohydrate	13 g
Dietary Fiber	1 g
Protein	4 g
Calcium	40 mg
Iron	<1 mg
Vitamin A	34 RE
Vitamin C	22 mg

DIETARY EXCHANGES:
½ Starch/Bread, 1 Vegetable

❖

Health Note

A daily dose of approximately 500 mg of sodium is required for the regulation of bodily functions. No upper limit has been established, yet most health experts recommend an intake of no more than 2,000-2,400 mg of sodium (about 1 teaspoon of salt) each day.

❖

FRENCH LENTIL SALAD

Balsamic vinegar and toasted walnuts add cosmopolitan flavor to the earthy taste of lentils.

¼ cup chopped walnuts
1½ cups dried lentils, rinsed, sorted and drained*
4 green onions, finely chopped
3 tablespoons balsamic vinegar
2 tablespoons chopped fresh parsley
1 tablespoon olive oil
¾ teaspoon salt
½ teaspoon dried thyme leaves
¼ teaspoon ground black pepper

1 Preheat oven to 375°F.

2 Spread walnuts in even layer in baking pan. Bake 5 minutes or until lightly browned, stirring occasionally. Remove from oven. Cool completely in baking pan.

3 Combine 2 quarts water and lentils in large saucepan; bring to a boil over high heat. Cover; reduce heat to medium-low. Simmer 30 minutes or until lentils are tender, stirring occasionally. Drain lentils; discard liquid.

4 Combine lentils, onions, vinegar, parsley, oil, salt, thyme and pepper in large bowl. Cover; refrigerate 1 hour or until cool.

5 Serve on lettuce leaves, if desired. Top each serving evenly with walnuts before serving. Garnish as desired.

Makes 4 servings

*Packages of dried lentils may contain grit and tiny stones. Therefore, thoroughly rinse lentils. Then sort through and discard grit or any unusual looking pieces.

Nutrients per Serving:

Calories	264
(28% of calories from fat)	
Total Fat	8 g
Saturated Fat	1 g
Cholesterol	0 mg
Sodium	406 mg
Carbohydrate	34 g
Dietary Fiber	8 g
Protein	16 g
Calcium	44 mg
Iron	6 mg
Vitamin A	39 RE
Vitamin C	9 mg

DIETARY EXCHANGES:
2 Starch/Bread, 1½ Lean Meat, ½ Fat

ROASTED CORN & WILD RICE SALAD

½ cup uncooked wild rice
1½ cups fresh whole kernel corn (about 3 medium ears)
½ cup chopped seeded tomato
½ cup finely chopped yellow or green bell pepper
⅓ cup chopped fresh cilantro
2 tablespoons minced seeded jalapeño peppers* (optional)
2 tablespoons fresh lime juice
2 tablespoons prepared honey mustard
1 tablespoon olive oil
½ teaspoon ground cumin

1 Place 1½ cups water in small saucepan; bring to a boil over high heat. Stir in wild rice; cover. Reduce heat to medium-low. Simmer 40 minutes or until rice is just tender but still firm to the bite. Drain rice; discard liquid.

2 Preheat oven to 400°F. Spray baking pan with nonstick cooking spray.

3 Spread corn evenly in prepared baking pan. Bake 20 to 25 minutes or until corn is lightly browned, stirring after 15 minutes.

4 Combine rice, corn, tomato, bell pepper, cilantro and jalapeños, if desired, in large bowl. Blend lime juice, honey mustard, oil and cumin in small bowl until smooth. Drizzle over rice mixture; toss to coat. Cover; refrigerate 2 hours before serving. Serve on lettuce leaves, if desired. *Makes 6 servings*

*Jalapeño peppers can sting and irritate the skin; wear rubber gloves when handling peppers and do not touch eyes.

The smoky-sweet taste of roasted corn adds robust flavor to the nutty overtones of wild rice. Both corn and wild rice are excellent sources of complex carbohydrates, which are broken down to glucose during digestion. The body is dependent on glucose for energy.

❖

Nutrients per Serving:

Calories	116
(20% of calories from fat)	
Total Fat	3 g
Saturated Fat	<1 g
Cholesterol	0 mg
Sodium	70 mg
Carbohydrate	21 g
Dietary Fiber	2 g
Protein	4 g
Calcium	16 mg
Iron	1 mg
Vitamin A	44 RE
Vitamin C	23 mg

DIETARY EXCHANGES: 1 Starch/Bread, 1 Vegetable, ½ Fat

ENTREES

BEEF & BEAN BURRITOS

Nonstick cooking spray
½ pound beef round steak, cut into ½-inch pieces
3 cloves garlic, minced
1 can (about 15 ounces) pinto beans, rinsed and drained
1 can (4 ounces) diced mild green chilies, drained
¼ cup chopped fresh cilantro
6 (6-inch) flour tortillas
½ cup (2 ounces) shredded reduced fat Cheddar cheese
Salsa (optional)

1 Spray nonstick skillet with cooking spray; heat over medium heat until hot. Add steak and garlic; cook and stir 5 minutes or until steak is cooked to desired doneness.

2 Add beans, chilies and cilantro to skillet; cook 5 minutes or until heated through, stirring occasionally.

3 Spoon steak mixture evenly down centers of tortillas; sprinkle cheese evenly over steak mixture. Top with salsa, if desired. Fold bottom ends of tortillas over filling; roll to enclose. Garnish with peppers, lettuce, green onions and nonfat sour cream, if desired.

Makes 6 servings

❖

Steak plays a supporting role in these easy-to-make burritos. It's the straightforward flavors of cilantro and green chilies that capture the essence of Mexican cuisine.

❖

Nutrients per Serving:

Calories	278
(22% of calories from fat)	
Total Fat	7 g
Saturated Fat	2 g
Cholesterol	31 mg
Sodium	956 mg
Carbohydrate	36 g
Dietary Fiber	1 g
Protein	19 g
Calcium	121 mg
Iron	2 mg
Vitamin A	48 RE
Vitamin C	23 mg

DIETARY EXCHANGES:
2 Starch/Bread, 1½ Lean Meat, 1 Vegetable, ½ Fat

SHRIMP AND SNOW PEAS WITH FUSILLI

❖

Shrimp star in this Mexican-inspired stir-fry. A 3-ounce serving of shrimp has more calcium than a 1-cup glass of milk. Calcium deficiencies are linked to colon cancer and hypertension.

❖

Nutrients per Serving:

Calories	228
(24% of calories from fat)	
Total Fat	6 g
Saturated Fat	1 g
Cholesterol	87 mg
Sodium	202 mg
Carbohydrate	29 g
Dietary Fiber	3 g
Protein	15 g
Calcium	52 mg
Iron	4 mg
Vitamin A	92 RE
Vitamin C	36 mg

DIETARY EXCHANGES:
1½ Starch/Bread, 1 Lean Meat, 1 Vegetable, 1 Fat

6 ounces uncooked fusilli
 Nonstick cooking spray
2 cloves garlic, minced
¼ teaspoon crushed red pepper
12 ounces medium shrimp, peeled and deveined
2 cups snow peas
1 can (8 ounces) sliced water chestnuts, drained
⅓ cup sliced green onions
3 tablespoons lime juice
2 tablespoons chopped fresh cilantro
2 tablespoons olive oil
1 tablespoon reduced sodium soy sauce
1½ teaspoons Mexican seasoning

1 Cook pasta according to package directions, omitting salt; drain. Set aside.

2 Spray large nonstick skillet with cooking spray; heat over medium heat until hot. Add garlic and red pepper; stir-fry 1 minute. Add shrimp; stir-fry 5 minutes or until shrimp are opaque. Remove shrimp from skillet.

3 Add snow peas and 2 tablespoons water to skillet; cook, covered, 1 minute. Uncover; cook and stir 2 minutes or until snow peas are crisp-tender. Remove snow peas from skillet.

4 Combine pasta, shrimp, snow peas, water chestnuts and onions in large bowl. Whisk lime juice, cilantro, oil, soy sauce and Mexican seasoning in small bowl until well blended. Drizzle over pasta mixture; toss to coat. Garnish with radishes, if desired.

Makes 6 servings

GREEK WHITE BEAN RISOTTO

❖

*Assorted flavor
combinations of feta cheese
are available in many
supermarkets. They taste
less pungent than the
traditional flavor of this
classic Greek cheese and
provide an exceptional
accent to this dish.*

❖

1 tablespoon low-sodium chicken flavor bouillon granules
   Nonstick cooking spray
3 cloves garlic, minced
1½ cups uncooked arborio rice
2 teaspoons dried oregano leaves
⅓ cup chopped solid-pack sun-dried tomatoes
1 cup rinsed, drained canned cannellini beans (white kidney beans)
¾ cup (3 ounces) crumbled feta cheese
⅓ cup shredded Parmesan cheese
1 teaspoon lemon juice
½ teaspoon ground black pepper

1 Combine 5½ cups water and bouillon granules in large saucepan; cover. Bring to a simmer over medium-low heat. Keep broth simmering by adjusting heat.

2 Spray large saucepan with cooking spray; heat over medium heat until hot. Add garlic; cook and stir 1 minute. Add rice and oregano; reduce heat to medium-low. Cook and stir 2 minutes.

3 Add 1 cup hot chicken broth to rice mixture; cook until broth is absorbed, stirring constantly. Stir another ½ cup hot chicken broth into rice mixture, stirring constantly until broth is absorbed. Stir in tomatoes.

4 Stir remaining hot chicken broth into rice mixture, ½ cup at a time, stirring constantly until all broth is absorbed before adding next ½ cup. (Total cooking time for chicken broth absorption is about 35 to 40 minutes or until rice is just tender but still firm to the bite.)

5 Add beans to saucepan; cook 1 minute, stirring constantly. Remove saucepan from heat. Stir in cheeses, lemon juice and pepper. Cover; let stand 5 minutes. Stir once. Serve with breadsticks, if desired. Garnish with oregano and red pepper cutout, if desired.

Makes 5 servings

Nutrients per Serving:

Calories	351
(17% of calories from fat)	
Total Fat	7 g
Saturated Fat	4 g
Cholesterol	20 mg
Sodium	831 mg
Carbohydrate	60 g
Dietary Fiber	3 g
Protein	13 g
Calcium	211 mg
Iron	4 mg
Vitamin A	235 RE
Vitamin C	6 mg

DIETARY EXCHANGES:
4 Starch/Bread, 1 Lean
Meat, ½ Fat

TURKEY VEGETABLE CHILI MAC

❖

Essential fatty acids abound in this scrumptious dish. They play a key role in the maintenance of healthy skin and are also involved in the regulation of cholesterol and blood pressure.

❖

Nutrients per Serving:

Calories	236
(21% of calories from fat)	
Total Fat	6 g
Saturated Fat	1 g
Cholesterol	25 mg
Sodium	445 mg
Carbohydrate	34 g
Dietary Fiber	6 g
Protein	17 g
Calcium	73 mg
Iron	2 mg
Vitamin A	151 RE
Vitamin C	22 mg

DIETARY EXCHANGES:
1½ Starch/Bread, 1 Lean Meat, 2 Vegetable, ½ Fat

Nonstick cooking spray
¾ pound ground turkey breast
½ cup chopped onion
2 cloves garlic, minced
1 can (about 15 ounces) black beans, rinsed and drained
1 can (14½ ounces) Mexican-style stewed tomatoes, undrained
1 can (14½ ounces) no-salt-added diced tomatoes, undrained
1 cup frozen whole kernel corn
1 teaspoon Mexican seasoning
½ cup uncooked elbow macaroni
⅓ cup reduced fat sour cream

1 Spray large nonstick saucepan with cooking spray; heat over medium heat until hot. Add turkey, onion and garlic; cook 5 minutes or until turkey is no longer pink, stirring to crumble.

2 Add beans, tomatoes with liquid, corn and Mexican seasoning to saucepan; bring to a boil over high heat, stirring occasionally. Cover; reduce heat to low. Simmer 15 minutes, stirring occasionally.

3 Meanwhile, cook pasta according to package directions, omitting salt; drain. Add to saucepan. Simmer 2 to 3 minutes or until heated through, stirring occasionally.

4 Top each serving evenly with sour cream. Garnish with fresh cilantro, cheese slices and tomatillos, if desired.

Makes 6 servings

SEAFOOD PAELLA

❖

Many paella recipes are prepared with as much as a half cup of oil. Here, oil is omitted, amounting to a savings of more than 150 calories from fat per serving.

❖

Nutrients per Serving:

Calories	340
(5% of calories from fat)	
Total Fat	2 g
Saturated Fat	<1 g
Cholesterol	132 mg
Sodium	570 mg
Carbohydrate	54 g
Dietary Fiber	5 g
Protein	27 g
Calcium	95 mg
Iron	6 mg
Vitamin A	101 RE
Vitamin C	43 mg

DIETARY EXCHANGES:
3 Starch/Bread, 2 Lean
Meat, 2 Vegetable

Nonstick cooking spray
1 cup chopped red bell pepper
⅔ cup chopped onion
1 tablespoon minced garlic
½ teaspoon ground turmeric
½ teaspoon paprika
2 teaspoons vegetable flavor bouillon granules
1½ cups uncooked medium grain white rice
1 cup frozen artichoke hearts, thawed, halved
1 pound medium shrimp, peeled and deveined, cut lengthwise in half
½ pound sea scallops, cut into quarters
¾ cup frozen baby lima beans, thawed
½ cup frozen sweet peas, thawed

1 Spray large heavy saucepan or Dutch oven with cooking spray; heat over medium-high heat until hot. Add bell pepper, onion and garlic; cook and stir 3 minutes or until vegetables are crisp-tender. Stir in turmeric and paprika; cook and stir 1 minute.

2 Add 3¼ cups water and bouillon granules to saucepan; bring to a boil over high heat. Stir in rice and artichoke hearts. Cover; reduce heat to medium-low. Simmer 18 minutes, stirring occasionally.

3 Add shrimp, scallops, beans and peas to saucepan; cover. Simmer 5 minutes or until seafood is opaque and liquid is absorbed. Remove saucepan from heat. Let stand 5 minutes before serving. Garnish with strips of red bell pepper and Italian parsley, if desired.

Makes 6 servings

DOUBLE PEA SOUP

This scrumptious pea soup doubles as a nutritional bargain. It's filled with hard-to-find nutrients including folate, iron, copper and magnesium.

1 tablespoon vegetable oil
1 large white onion, finely chopped
3 cloves garlic, minced
2 cups dried split peas*
1 bay leaf
1 teaspoon ground mustard
1½ cups frozen green peas
1 teaspoon salt
¼ teaspoon ground black pepper

1 Heat oil in large saucepan or Dutch oven over medium-high heat until hot. Add onion; cook 5 minutes or until onion is tender, stirring occasionally. Add garlic; cook and stir 2 minutes.

2 Add 2 cups water, split peas, bay leaf and mustard to saucepan. Bring to a boil over high heat, stirring occasionally. Cover; reduce heat to medium-low. Simmer 45 minutes or until split peas are tender, stirring occasionally.

3 Add green peas, salt and pepper to saucepan; cover. Cook 10 minutes or until green peas are tender. Remove and discard bay leaf. Blend soup using hand-held blender until smooth. Or, process small batches of soup in blender or food processor until smooth.

4 Garnish with additional green peas, yellow bell pepper cutouts and sour cream, if desired.

Makes 6 servings

*Packages of dried beans may contain grit and tiny stones. Therefore, thoroughly rinse beans. Then sort through and discard grit or any unusual looking pieces.

Note: If a smoky flavor is desired, a chipotle chili can be added during the last 5 minutes of cooking.

Nutrients per Serving:

Calories	290
(10% of calories from fat)	
Total Fat	3 g
Saturated Fat	<1 g
Cholesterol	0 mg
Sodium	401 mg
Carbohydrate	48 g
Dietary Fiber	5 g
Protein	19 g
Calcium	59 mg
Iron	4 mg
Vitamin A	37 RE
Vitamin C	7 mg

DIETARY EXCHANGES:
3 Starch/Bread, 1 Lean Meat, ½ Vegetable

TURKEY SHANGHAI

Angel hair pasta adds a wonderful twist to this Oriental favorite.

Nonstick cooking spray
¾ pound turkey breast tenderloin, thinly sliced
1 cup thinly sliced carrots
½ cup sliced green onions
3 cloves garlic, minced
4 cups ⅓-less-salt chicken broth
6 ounces uncooked angel hair pasta
2 cups frozen French-style green beans
¼ cup plus 2 tablespoons stir-fry sauce
1 teaspoon Oriental sesame oil

1 Spray large nonstick skillet with cooking spray; heat over medium heat until hot. Add turkey and carrots; cook and stir 5 minutes or until turkey is no longer pink. Add onions and garlic; cook and stir 2 minutes.

2 Add chicken broth to skillet; bring to a boil over high heat. Add pasta. Return to a boil. Reduce heat to medium-low. Simmer 5 minutes, stirring occasionally.

3 Add green beans to skillet. Simmer 2 to 3 minutes or until pasta is just tender, stirring occasionally. Remove skillet from heat. Stir in stir-fry sauce and oil. Let stand 5 minutes before serving. Garnish with carrot cutout, fresh herbs and slice of radish.

Makes 6 servings

Nutrients per Serving:

Calories	216
(15% of calories from fat)	
Total Fat	4 g
Saturated Fat	1 g
Cholesterol	25 mg
Sodium	712 mg
Carbohydrate	28 g
Dietary Fiber	3 g
Protein	19 g
Calcium	43 mg
Iron	2 mg
Vitamin A	577 RE
Vitamin C	9 mg

DIETARY EXCHANGES:
1½ Starch/Bread, 1½ Lean Meat, 1 Vegetable

❖ Cook's Tip

When purchasing green onions, choose those with crisp, bright green tips and a firm white base. Store unwashed green onions in an airtight container for up to 5 days in the refrigerator.

❖

INDIAN CHICKEN WITH COUSCOUS

❖

The seasonings combine deliciously and impart a mildly spicy flavor to this quick-to-fix dish.

❖

Nutrients per Serving:

Calories	505
(11% of calories from fat)	
Total Fat	6 g
Saturated Fat	1 g
Cholesterol	66 mg
Sodium	378 mg
Carbohydrate	76 g
Dietary Fiber	13 g
Protein	37 g
Calcium	150 mg
Iron	3 mg
Vitamin A	156 RE
Vitamin C	70 mg

DIETARY EXCHANGES:
3 Starch/Bread, 3 Lean
Meat, 1 Fruit, 3 Vegetable

1 pound boneless skinless chicken breasts
2 teaspoons olive oil
1 cup chopped onion
1 cup chopped green bell pepper
1 teaspoon chili powder
1 teaspoon curry powder
½ teaspoon ground red pepper
1 can (14½ ounces) Mexican-style stewed tomatoes, undrained
⅓ cup golden raisins
1⅓ cups ⅓-less-salt chicken broth
1⅓ cups uncooked quick-cooking couscous
½ cup plain nonfat yogurt
¼ cup sliced green onions

1 Cut chicken lengthwise into ¼-inch-thick slices; cut each slice into 1-inch strips.

2 Heat oil in large nonstick skillet over medium-high heat until hot. Add chicken; cook and stir 5 minutes or until chicken is no longer pink. Remove chicken from skillet; set aside.

3 Add onion, bell pepper, chili powder, curry powder and red pepper to skillet; cook and stir 5 minutes or until vegetables are tender.

4 Add chicken, tomatoes with liquid and raisins to skillet; bring to a boil over high heat, stirring occasionally. Cover; reduce heat to medium-low. Simmer 15 minutes. Uncover; simmer 5 minutes, stirring occasionally.

5 Meanwhile, place chicken broth in small saucepan; bring to a boil over high heat. Stir in couscous; cover. Remove saucepan from heat; let stand 5 minutes.

6 Serve chicken mixture over couscous. Top each serving with 2 tablespoons yogurt and 1 tablespoon green onions. Garnish with fresh herbs, if desired.

Makes 4 servings

SHRIMP WITH SPICY BLACK BEAN SAUCE

❖

Black beans, popular in Cuban and Mexican fare, team up with the Orient in this spicy sauce. For an exciting variation, omit the shrimp and serve this smashingly good sauce over chicken or fish.

❖

Nutrients per Serving:

Calories	297
(15% of calories from fat)	
Total Fat	5 g
Saturated Fat	1 g
Cholesterol	174 mg
Sodium	562 mg
Carbohydrate	36 g
Dietary Fiber	2 g
Protein	26 g
Calcium	63 mg
Iron	5 mg
Vitamin A	102 RE

DIETARY EXCHANGES:
2½ Starch/Bread, 2 Lean Meat

1 can (about 15 ounces) black beans, rinsed and drained
1 tablespoon peanut oil
1 tablespoon minced fresh ginger
2 cloves garlic, minced
¼ teaspoon crushed red pepper
1 pound medium shrimp, peeled with tails left on and deveined
½ cup chicken broth
2 teaspoons cornstarch
2 tablespoons reduced sodium soy sauce
1 tablespoon rice wine vinegar
4 green onions, chopped
2 cups hot, cooked white rice

1 Place beans in medium bowl; mash with fork or potato masher until smooth.

2 Heat oil in large wok or nonstick skillet over medium-high heat until hot. Add ginger, garlic and red pepper; stir-fry 1 minute. Add beans, shrimp and chicken broth to wok. Cook and stir 2 minutes.

3 Blend cornstarch, soy sauce and vinegar in small bowl until smooth; add to wok. Cook and stir 2 minutes. Add onions; cook and stir 1 minute or until shrimp are opaque and sauce thickens.

4 Serve over hot, cooked rice. Garnish with strips of carrot and zucchini.

Makes 4 servings

CHEESE RAVIOLI WITH PUMPKIN SAUCE

For a delicious variation, add cooked shrimp to the pumpkin sauce and serve over your favorite pasta.

❖

Nutrients per Serving:

Calories	270
(7% of calories from fat)	
Total Fat	2 g
Saturated Fat	1 g
Cholesterol	6 mg
Sodium	556 mg
Carbohydrate	45 g
Dietary Fiber	1 g
Protein	18 g
Calcium	135 mg
Iron	1 mg
Vitamin A	522 RE
Vitamin C	4 mg

DIETARY EXCHANGES:
2½ Starch/Bread, 1 Lean Meat, ½ Milk

Nonstick cooking spray
⅓ cup sliced green onions
1 to 2 cloves garlic, minced
½ teaspoon fennel seeds
1 cup evaporated skim milk
1 tablespoon all-purpose flour
¼ teaspoon salt
⅛ teaspoon ground black pepper
½ cup solid pack pumpkin
2 packages (9 ounces each) refrigerated low fat cheese ravioli
2 tablespoons grated Parmesan cheese (optional)

1 Spray medium nonstick saucepan with cooking spray; heat over medium heat until hot. Add onions, garlic and fennel seeds; cook and stir 3 minutes or until onions are tender.

2 Whisk milk, flour, salt and pepper in small bowl until smooth; add to saucepan. Bring to a boil over high heat, stirring constantly. Boil 5 minutes or until thickened, stirring constantly. Stir in pumpkin; reduce heat to low.

3 Meanwhile, cook ravioli according to package directions, omitting salt. Rinse; drain. Divide ravioli evenly among 6 plates. Spoon sauce and sprinkle cheese, if desired, evenly over each serving. Serve immediately. Garnish with grapes and orange slices, if desired.

Makes 6 servings

HEARTY CASSOULET

Cassoulet, a stew of beans baked with high fat, high sodium meats such as sausage and pork rind, is a French country classic. This version gets low fat countryside flavor from turkey sausage and skinless chicken thighs.

1 tablespoon olive oil
1 large onion, finely chopped
4 boneless skinless chicken thighs (about 1 pound), chopped
¼ pound smoked turkey sausage, finely chopped
3 cloves garlic, minced
3 cans (about 15 ounces each) Great Northern beans, rinsed and drained
¼ cup fresh tomato paste
1 teaspoon dried thyme leaves
½ teaspoon ground black pepper
½ cup fresh bread crumbs
3 tablespoons chopped fresh parsley

1 Heat oil in ovenproof Dutch oven over medium-high heat until hot. Add onion; cook and stir 5 minutes or until onion is tender. Add chicken, sausage and garlic; cook 5 minutes or until chicken and sausage are browned, stirring occasionally.

2 Add beans, ¼ cup water, tomato paste, thyme and pepper to Dutch oven. Cover; reduce heat to medium-low. Simmer 15 minutes or until mixture is bubbly, stirring occasionally.

3 Preheat broiler. Combine bread crumbs and parsley in small bowl; sprinkle over top of cassoulet. Broil, 4 inches from heat, 3 minutes or until bread crumbs are lightly browned.

Makes 6 servings

Nutrients per Serving:

Calories	432
(18% of calories from fat)	
Total Fat	9 g
Saturated Fat	2 g
Cholesterol	45 mg
Sodium	365 mg
Carbohydrate	59 g
Dietary Fiber	1 g
Protein	31 g
Calcium	176 mg
Iron	6 mg
Vitamin A	44 RE
Vitamin C	12 mg

DIETARY EXCHANGES:
3½ Starch/Bread, 3 Lean Meat, 1 Vegetable

Health Note

While a calcium-rich meal plan and plenty of vitamin D play a role in the prevention of osteoporosis, so does exercise. Research has shown that weight-bearing exercise, such as walking and running, provides an excellent defense against the development of this bone-thinning disease.

LEMONY DILL SALMON AND SHELL CASSEROLE

❖

Bone up on calcium with each serving of this refreshing casserole. Good-for-your-bones calcium may also keep high blood pressure levels in check. High blood pressure is one of the leading causes of strokes.

❖

Nutrients per Serving:

Calories	233
(15% of calories from fat)	
Total Fat	4 g
Saturated Fat	1 g
Cholesterol	17 mg
Sodium	362 mg
Carbohydrate	33 g
Dietary Fiber	3 g
Protein	17 g
Calcium	209 mg
Iron	3 mg
Vitamin A	122 RE
Vitamin C	9 mg

DIETARY EXCHANGES:
2 Starch/Bread, 1 Lean Meat, ½ Milk

6 ounces uncooked medium shell pasta
Nonstick cooking spray
1½ cups sliced mushrooms
⅓ cup sliced green onions
1 clove garlic, minced
2 cups skim milk
3 tablespoons all-purpose flour
1 tablespoon grated lemon peel
¾ teaspoon dried dill weed
¼ teaspoon salt
⅛ teaspoon ground black pepper
1½ cups frozen green peas
1 can (7½ ounces) salmon, drained and flaked

1 Preheat oven to 350°F. Cook pasta according to package directions, omitting salt; drain. Rinse and drain again. Set aside.

2 Spray medium nonstick saucepan with cooking spray; heat over medium heat until hot. Add mushrooms, onions and garlic; cook and stir 5 minutes or until vegetables are tender.

3 Blend milk and flour in medium bowl until smooth. Stir in lemon peel, dill weed, salt and pepper. Add to saucepan; heat over medium-high heat 5 to 8 minutes or until thickened, stirring constantly. Remove saucepan from heat. Stir in pasta, peas and salmon; blend well. Spoon pasta mixture into 2-quart casserole.

4 Bake, covered, 35 to 40 minutes. Serve immediately. Garnish with lemon wedges and fresh dill.

Makes 6 servings

WHITE CHILI PILAF

❖

The unique flavors of this tasty dish blend well with any lean meat or poultry.

❖

Nonstick cooking spray
½ pound lean ground beef
½ pound bulk turkey sausage
1 cup finely chopped green bell pepper
2 to 3 tablespoons seeded, minced jalapeño peppers*
2 teaspoons minced garlic
2 teaspoons ground cumin
½ teaspoon dried oregano leaves
2 teaspoons chicken flavor bouillon granules
1 cup uncooked white basmati rice
1 cup rinsed, drained canned Great Northern beans
1 cup sliced green onions
½ cup chopped fresh cilantro
6 tablespoons nonfat sour cream
¾ cup diced seeded tomato
½ cup plus 1 tablespoon shredded reduced fat Monterey Jack and Colby cheese

Nutrients per Serving:

Calories	324
(26% of calories from fat)	
Total Fat	10 g
Saturated Fat	3 g
Cholesterol	50 mg
Sodium	731 mg
Carbohydrate	41 g
Dietary Fiber	1 g
Protein	20 g
Calcium	71 mg
Iron	5 mg
Vitamin A	109 RE
Vitamin C	48 mg

DIETARY EXCHANGES:
2½ Starch/Bread, 2 Lean Mean, 1 Vegetable, ½ Fat

1 Spray large nonstick skillet with cooking spray; heat over medium heat until hot. Add beef and sausage; cook 5 minutes or until meat is no longer pink, stirring to crumble. Remove meat from skillet. Set aside.

2 Spray large saucepan with cooking spray; heat over medium-high heat until hot. Add peppers and garlic. Cook and stir over medium heat 5 minutes or until peppers are tender. Stir in cumin and oregano; cook and stir 1 minute. Stir in 2¼ cups water and bouillon granules; bring to a boil over high heat. Stir in rice. Cover; reduce heat to medium-low. Simmer 15 minutes.

3 Add meat, beans and onions to saucepan; cover. Simmer 5 minutes or until rice is tender. Remove saucepan from heat; stir in cilantro. Cover; let stand 5 minutes. Top each serving evenly with sour cream, tomato and cheese. Serve immediately.

Makes 6 servings

*Jalapeño peppers can sting and irritate the skin; wear rubber gloves when handling peppers and do not touch eyes.

PASTA AND TUNA FILLED PEPPERS

Add pizzazz to this bell pepper dish—serve each salad in a different color pepper. The colors will jazz up the table and the flavorful filling will excite your taste buds.

Nutrients per Serving:

Calories	216
(16% of calories from fat)	
Total Fat	4 g
Saturated Fat	1 g
Cholesterol	26 mg
Sodium	574 mg
Carbohydrate	27 g
Dietary Fiber	2 g
Protein	19 g
Calcium	123 mg
Iron	2 mg
Vitamin A	124 RE
Vitamin C	78 mg

DIETARY EXCHANGES: 1 Starch/Bread, 2 Lean Meat, 1½ Vegetable

¾ cup uncooked ditalini pasta
4 large green bell peppers*
1 cup chopped seeded tomato
1 can (6⅛ ounces) white tuna packed in water, drained and flaked
½ cup chopped celery
½ cup (2 ounces) shredded reduced fat Cheddar cheese
¼ cup fat free mayonnaise or salad dressing
1 teaspoon salt-free garlic and herb seasoning

1 Cook pasta according to package directions, omitting salt; drain. Rinse and drain again. Set aside.

2 Cut thin slice from top of each pepper. Remove veins and seeds from insides of peppers. Rinse; place peppers cut side down on paper towels to drain.

3 Combine pasta, tomato, tuna, celery, ½ cup cheese, mayonnaise and seasoning in large bowl until well blended; spoon into pepper shells.

4 Place peppers on large microwave-safe plate; cover with waxed paper. Microwave at HIGH 8 minutes or until heated through, turning halfway through cooking time.

5 Sprinkle additional cheese evenly over each serving, if desired. Garnish with fresh greens and herbs, if desired.

Makes 4 servings

*For tender peppers, cook in boiling water 2 minutes. Rinse with cold water; drain upside down on paper towels before filling.

VEGETABLE & PASTA PAELLA

❖

Portobella mushrooms and orzo pasta masquerade as meat and rice in this Spanish one-dish favorite. Although lacking in meat, this dish serves up 25 percent of the RDA for iron. Vitamin C, also abundant in this dish, helps the body absorb iron.

❖

Nonstick cooking spray
1 cup chopped onion
¾ cup chopped green bell pepper
2 cloves garlic, minced
1½ cups sliced portobella mushrooms or any variety mushrooms
2 cups ⅓-less-salt chicken broth
1 can (14½ ounces) Mexican-style stewed tomatoes, undrained
1 teaspoon chili powder
1 teaspoon paprika
½ teaspoon ground cumin
⅛ teaspoon ground black pepper
¾ cup uncooked orzo pasta
1 can (about 15 ounces) garbanzo beans (chick-peas), rinsed and drained
1 cup frozen green peas, thawed

1 Spray large nonstick skillet or Dutch oven with cooking spray; heat over medium heat until hot. Add onion, bell pepper and garlic; cook and stir 5 minutes or until vegetables are tender. Add mushrooms; cook and stir 1 minute.

2 Add chicken broth, tomatoes with liquid, chili powder, paprika, cumin and black pepper to skillet; bring to a boil over high heat, stirring occasionally. Add pasta. Cover; reduce heat to medium-low. Simmer, 15 minutes, stirring occasionally to prevent pasta from sticking to bottom of skillet.

3 Add beans and peas to skillet; bring to a boil over high heat. Reduce heat to low. Simmer 5 minutes, stirring frequently. Serve immediately. Garnish with sprigs of fresh rosemary and thyme, if desired.

Makes 6 servings

Nutrients per Serving:

Calories	247
(11% of calories from fat)	
Total Fat	3 g
Saturated Fat	<1 g
Cholesterol	0 mg
Sodium	622 mg
Carbohydrate	46 g
Dietary Fiber	8 g
Protein	12 g
Calcium	78 mg
Iron	5 mg
Vitamin A	116 RE
Vitamin C	44 mg

DIETARY EXCHANGES: 3 Starch/Bread, 2 Vegetable, ½ Fat

SIDE DISHES

SPICED MUSHROOM PECAN RICE TIMBALES

Basmati rice, cooked with flavorful cinnamon and allspice, is packed into custard cups and unmolded onto dinner plates just prior to serving. The fruity overtones of this elegant dish are wonderful alongside honey-glazed pork tenderloin or ham.

Nonstick cooking spray
¼ cup toasted pecans
1 cup chopped shiitake or other mushrooms
¾ cup apple juice
1 (3-inch) cinnamon stick, broken in half
¼ teaspoon salt
3 whole allspice
¾ cup uncooked white basmati rice
3 tablespoons chopped fresh chives or green onions

1 Preheat oven to 375°F. Spray 5 (5-ounce) custard cups or molds with cooking spray; set aside.

2 Spread pecans in even layer in baking pan. Bake 5 minutes or until lightly browned, stirring occasionally. Cool completely in pan.

3 Spray heavy, medium saucepan with cooking spray; heat over medium-high heat until hot. Add mushrooms; cook and stir 5 minutes or until tender.

4 Add ¾ cup water, apple juice, cinnamon sticks, salt and allspice to saucepan; bring to a boil over high heat. Stir in rice; cover. Reduce heat to medium-low. Simmer 15 to 20 minutes or until liquid is absorbed and rice is tender. Remove saucepan from heat. Remove and discard cinnamon sticks and allspice. Stir in pecans and chives.

5 Spoon rice mixture evenly into prepared cups; pack down with back of spoon. Let stand 5 minutes; unmold onto serving plates. Serve immediately. Garnish with fresh fruit and strips of green onions, if desired.

Makes 5 servings

Nutrients per Serving:

Calories	175
(20% of calories from fat)	
Total Fat	4 g
Saturated Fat	<1 g
Cholesterol	0 mg
Sodium	109 mg
Carbohydrate	33 g
Dietary Fiber	1 g
Protein	3 g
Calcium	10 mg
Iron	2 mg
Vitamin A	8 RE
Vitamin C	17 mg

DIETARY EXCHANGES:
2 Starch/Bread, ½ Fat

BLACK BEAN CAKES WITH SALSA CRUDA

❖

For a scrumptious variation, serve these bean cakes on whole grain buns with low fat Cheddar cheese, salsa and nonfat sour cream.

❖

Nutrients per Serving:

Calories	145
(9% of calories from fat)	
Total Fat	2 g
Saturated Fat	<1 g
Cholesterol	<1 mg
Sodium	415 mg
Carbohydrate	30 g
Dietary Fiber	8 g
Protein	11 g
Calcium	33 mg
Iron	1 mg
Vitamin A	118 RE
Vitamin C	16 mg

DIETARY EXCHANGES:
2 Starch/Bread

Salsa Cruda (recipe follows)
1 can (about 15 ounces) black beans, rinsed and drained
¼ cup all-purpose flour
¼ cup chopped fresh cilantro
2 tablespoons plain low fat yogurt
1 tablespoon chili powder
2 cloves garlic, minced
Nonstick cooking spray

1 Prepare Salsa Cruda.

2 Place beans in medium bowl; mash with fork or potato masher until almost smooth, leaving some beans in larger pieces. Add flour, cilantro, yogurt, chili powder and garlic; blend well.

3 Spray large nonstick skillet with cooking spray; heat over medium-high heat until hot. For each cake, drop 2 heaping tablespoonsful bean mixture onto skillet; flatten to form cake with back of wooden spoon. Cook 6 to 8 minutes or until lightly browned, turning once. Serve with Salsa Cruda. Garnish with lime wedges, pepper and fresh cilantro, if desired. *Makes 4 servings*

SALSA CRUDA

1 cup chopped tomato
2 tablespoons finely chopped onion
2 tablespoons chopped fresh cilantro (optional)
2 tablespoons lime juice
½ jalapeño pepper, seeded, minced*
1 clove garlic, minced

1 Combine all ingredients in small bowl. Cover with plastic wrap. Refrigerate 1 hour. Bring to room temperature before serving. *Makes 4 servings*

*Jalapeño peppers can sting and irritate the skin; wear rubber gloves when handling peppers and do not touch eyes.

LEMON BROCCOLI PASTA

❖

Lemon adds a tangy yet refreshing flavor to this creamy side dish. It's absolutely delicious served with lean beef tenderloin.

❖

Nonstick cooking spray
3 tablespoons sliced green onions
1 clove garlic, minced
2 cups ⅓-less-salt chicken broth
1½ teaspoons grated lemon peel
⅛ teaspoon ground black pepper
2 cups thawed frozen or fresh broccoli flowerets
3 ounces uncooked angel hair pasta
⅓ cup low fat sour cream
2 tablespoons grated Parmesan cheese

1 Spray large nonstick saucepan with cooking spray; heat over medium heat until hot. Add onions and garlic; cook and stir 3 minutes or until onions are tender.

2 Add chicken broth, lemon peel and pepper to saucepan; bring to a boil over high heat. Add broccoli and pasta; return to a boil. Reduce heat to medium-low. Simmer 6 to 7 minutes or until pasta is tender, stirring frequently.

3 Remove saucepan from heat. Add sour cream; blend well. Let stand 5 minutes before serving. Top each serving with cheese. Garnish as desired.

Makes 6 servings

Nutrients per Serving:

Calories	100
(20% of calories from fat)	
Total Fat	2 g
Saturated Fat	<1 g
Cholesterol	6 mg
Sodium	176 mg
Carbohydrate	14 g
Dietary Fiber	3 g
Protein	7 g
Calcium	82 mg
Iron	1 mg
Vitamin A	186 RE
Vitamin C	27 mg

DIETARY EXCHANGES:
½ Starch/Bread, 1½ Vegetable, ½ Fat

❖

Cook's Tip
When buying broccoli, choose stalks with dark green heads that are tinged with purple. Store unwashed broccoli in an airtight container for up to 4 days in the refrigerator.

❖

CURRIED LENTILS WITH FRUIT

❖

Curry powder, apples and raisins transform this humble dish of lentils into an exotic side for meats and poultry.

❖

Nutrients per Serving:

Calories	160
(3% of calories from fat)	
Total Fat	1 g
Saturated Fat	<1 g
Cholesterol	<1 mg
Sodium	364 mg
Carbohydrate	31 g
Dietary Fiber	6 g
Protein	10 g
Calcium	44 mg
Iron	4 mg
Vitamin A	3 RE
Vitamin C	3 mg

DIETARY EXCHANGES:
2 Starch/Bread, ½ Fruit

1½ cups uncooked lentils, rinsed, sorted and drained*
1 Granny Smith apple, cored, peeled and chopped
¼ cup golden raisins
¼ cup lemon nonfat yogurt
1 teaspoon curry powder
1 teaspoon salt

1 Combine 2 quarts water and lentils in large saucepan; bring to a boil over high heat. Reduce heat to medium-low. Simmer 20 minutes, stirring occasionally.

2 Add apple and raisins to saucepan; cook 10 minutes or until lentils are tender, stirring occasionally. Drain.

3 Combine lentil mixture, yogurt, curry powder and salt in large serving bowl until well blended. Garnish with lettuce, radishes and yellow bell peppers, if desired.

Makes 6 servings

*Packages of dried lentils may contain grit and tiny stones. Therefore, thoroughly rinse lentils. Then sort through and discard grit or any unusual looking pieces.

❖

Cook's Tip
Apples brown easily once they are cut. To prevent undesirable browning, sprinkle lemon, apple or grapefruit juice over apple pieces.

❖

GREEN BEAN RICE ALMONDINE

❖

*Colorful green beans
combine with rice in this
extra-easy twist on a classic.
Decrease preparation time
even more by substituting
frozen French-style green
beans for fresh green beans.*

❖

3 tablespoons sliced almonds, toasted
2 tablespoons reduced calorie margarine
½ cup finely chopped onion
1¼ cups ⅓-less-salt chicken broth
½ teaspoon lemon pepper seasoning
1 cup diagonally sliced green beans
1¼ cups uncooked instant white rice

1 Preheat oven to 375°F.

2 Spread almonds in even layer on baking pan. Bake 5 minutes or until lightly browned, stirring occasionally. Cool completely on pan.

3 Melt margarine in medium saucepan over medium heat; add onion. Cook and stir 5 minutes or until onion is tender. Add chicken broth and lemon pepper seasoning; bring to a boil over high heat. Add beans; cover. Reduce heat to low. Simmer 7 minutes or until beans are tender, stirring occasionally.

4 Stir rice into saucepan; cover. Remove saucepan from heat. Let stand 5 minutes or until liquid is absorbed and rice is tender. Fluff rice mixture with fork; stir in almonds until well blended. Serve immediately. Garnish with lemon wedges and fresh basil leaves, if desired.

Makes 6 servings

Nutrients per Serving:	
Calories	128
(28% of calories from fat)	
Total Fat	4 g
Saturated Fat	1 g
Cholesterol	0 mg
Sodium	53 mg
Carbohydrate	20 g
Dietary Fiber	1 g
Protein	3 g
Calcium	28 mg
Iron	1 mg
Vitamin A	57 RE
Vitamin C	3 mg

DIETARY EXCHANGES:
1 Starch/Bread,
1 Vegetable, ½ Fat

EASY DILLED SUCCOTASH

1½ cups frozen lima beans
1 small onion, finely chopped
1½ cups frozen whole kernel corn, thawed
1 teaspoon salt
1 teaspoon sugar
1 teaspoon dried dill weed

1 Bring ½ cup water in medium saucepan to a boil over high heat. Add beans and onion; cover. Reduce heat to medium-low. Simmer 8 minutes.

2 Add corn to saucepan; cover. Simmer 5 minutes or until vegetables are tender. Drain bean mixture; discard liquid.

3 Place bean mixture in serving bowl; add salt, sugar and dill weed; blend well. Garnish with fresh parsley, if desired.

Makes 4 servings

❖

This simple duo of lima beans and corn has a delightfully upbeat flavor. It's loaded with vitamin E which, along with selenium and other antioxidants, works to neutralize harmful substances, such as smog and cigarette smoke, that have damaging effects on our cells.

❖

Nutrients per Serving:

Calories	126
(2% of calories from fat)	
Total Fat	<1 g
Saturated Fat	<1 g
Cholesterol	0 mg
Sodium	571 mg
Carbohydrate	28 g
Dietary Fiber	5 g
Protein	6 g
Calcium	28 mg
Iron	1 mg
Vitamin A	27 RE
Vitamin C	11 mg

DIETARY EXCHANGES:
2 Starch/Bread

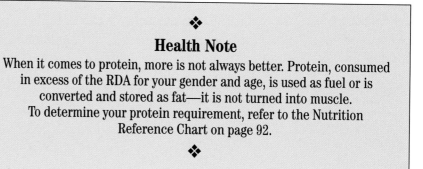

❖

Health Note

When it comes to protein, more is not always better. Protein, consumed in excess of the RDA for your gender and age, is used as fuel or is converted and stored as fat—it is not turned into muscle.
To determine your protein requirement, refer to the Nutrition Reference Chart on page 92.

❖

SPINACH PARMESAN RISOTTO

3⅔ cups ⅓-less-salt chicken broth
½ teaspoon ground white pepper
　　Nonstick cooking spray
1 cup uncooked arborio rice
1½ cups chopped fresh spinach
½ cup fresh or frozen green peas
1 tablespoon chopped fresh dill *or* 1 teaspoon dried dill weed
½ cup grated Parmesan cheese
1 teaspoon grated lemon peel

1 Combine chicken broth and pepper in medium saucepan; cover. Bring to a simmer over medium-low heat. Keep broth simmering by adjusting heat.

2 Spray large saucepan with cooking spray; heat over medium-low heat until hot. Add rice; cook and stir 1 minute. Stir ⅔ cup hot chicken broth into saucepan; cook, stirring constantly until broth is absorbed.

3 Stir remaining hot chicken broth into rice mixture, ½ cup at a time, stirring constantly until all broth is absorbed before adding next ½ cup. When last ½ cup chicken broth is added, stir spinach, peas and dill into saucepan. Cook, stirring gently until all broth is absorbed and rice is just tender but still firm to the bite. (Total cooking time for chicken broth absorption is about 35 to 40 minutes.)

4 Remove saucepan from heat; stir in cheese and lemon peel. Garnish with slice of lemon and fresh herbs, if desired.

Makes 6 servings

❖

This creamy risotto is packed with calcium and vitamin A. Calcium, which may protect against the development of osteoporosis, may also play a role in the prevention of colon cancer. Vitamin A may prevent the development of cancer as well by boosting the power of the immune system.

❖

Nutrients per Serving:

Calories	179
(15% of calories from fat)	
Total Fat	3 g
Saturated Fat	2 g
Cholesterol	7 mg
Sodium	198 mg
Carbohydrate	30 g
Dietary Fiber	1 g
Protein	7 g
Calcium	139 mg
Iron	2 mg
Vitamin A	121 RE
Vitamin C	6 mg

DIETARY EXCHANGES:
2 Starch/Bread, ½ Lean Meat

VEGETABLES WITH SPINACH FETTUCCINE

❖

Sun-dried tomatoes and florentine fettuccine turn everyday vegetables into a satisfying accompaniment to grilled poultry or fish.

❖

Nutrients per Serving:

Calories	82
(30% of calories from fat)	
Total Fat	3 g
Saturated Fat	<1 g
Cholesterol	3 mg
Sodium	101 mg
Carbohydrate	13 g
Dietary Fiber	1 g
Protein	3 g
Calcium	16 mg
Iron	1 mg
Vitamin A	280 RE
Vitamin C	16 mg

DIETARY EXCHANGES:
½ Starch/Bread, 1 Vegetable, ½ Fat

6 solid-pack sun-dried tomatoes
3 ounces uncooked spinach florentine fettuccine or spinach fettuccine
1 tablespoon olive oil
¼ cup chopped onion
¼ cup sliced red bell pepper
1 clove garlic, minced
½ cup sliced mushrooms
½ cup coarsely chopped fresh spinach
¼ teaspoon salt
¼ teaspoon ground nutmeg
⅛ teaspoon ground black pepper

1 Place sun-dried tomatoes in small bowl; pour boiling water over tomatoes to cover. Let stand 10 to 15 minutes or until tomatoes are tender. Drain tomatoes; discard liquid. Cut tomatoes into strips.

2 Cook pasta according to package directions, omitting salt; drain.

3 Heat oil in large nonstick skillet over medium heat until hot. Add onion, bell pepper and garlic; cook and stir 3 minutes or until vegetables are crisp-tender. Add mushrooms and spinach; cook and stir 1 minute. Add tomatoes, pasta, salt, nutmeg and black pepper; cook and stir 1 to 2 minutes or until heated through. Garnish with fresh herbs, if desired.

Makes 6 servings

POLENTA WITH BLACK BEAN SALSA

❖

This scrumptious side can be heated on the grill making it the perfect complement to grilled lean meats and poultry.

❖

Nutrients per Serving:

Calories	136
(24% of calories from fat)	
Total Fat	4 g
Saturated Fat	<1 g
Cholesterol	1 mg
Sodium	639 mg
Carbohydrate	23 g
Dietary Fiber	5 g
Protein	6 g
Calcium	28 mg
Iron	1 mg
Vitamin A	117 RE
Vitamin C	11 mg

DIETARY EXCHANGES:
1½ Starch/Bread, ½ Fat

Olive oil flavored nonstick cooking spray
2 teaspoons chicken flavor bouillon granules
¾ cup uncooked stone ground cornmeal or polenta
1 cup rinsed, drained canned black beans
¾ cup chunky salsa
⅔ cup frozen whole kernel corn, thawed
⅓ cup chopped fresh cilantro
4 teaspoons olive oil
6 tablespoons nonfat sour cream

1 Spray 9-inch square baking pan with cooking spray; set aside.

2 Combine 3 cups water and bouillon granules in large saucepan; bring to a boil over high heat. Gradually add cornmeal, stirring constantly with wire whisk. Reduce heat to medium-low. Simmer 10 to 15 minutes or until cornmeal is thickened and pulls away from side of pan, stirring constantly with wooden spoon.

3 Spread polenta evenly into prepared pan. Cover with plastic wrap; refrigerate 1 to 2 hours or until polenta is firm.

4 Combine beans, salsa, corn and cilantro in medium bowl. Cover with plastic wrap; refrigerate 1 hour. Bring to room temperature before serving.

5 Cut polenta into 6 rectangles; cut each rectangle diagonally to form 2 triangles. Brush both sides of triangles with oil. Spray large nonstick skillet with cooking spray; heat over medium-high heat until hot. Cook triangles, 4 at a time, 6 to 8 minutes or until browned, turning once.

6 Place 2 polenta triangles on each serving plate; top each serving evenly with black bean salsa and sour cream. Garnish as desired.

Makes 6 servings

Personalized Nutrition Reference for Different Calorie Levels*

Daily Calorie Level	1,600	2,000	2,200	2,800
Total Fat	53 g	65 g	73 g	93 g
% of Calories from Fat	30%	30%	30%	30%
Saturated Fat	18 g	20 g	24 g	31 g
Carbohydrate	240 g	300 g	330 g	420 g
Protein	46 g**	50 g	55 g	70 g
Dietary Fiber	20 g***	25 g	25 g	32 g
Cholesterol	300 mg	300 mg	300 mg	300 mg
Sodium	2,400 mg	2,400 mg	2,400 mg	2,400 mg
Calcium	1,000 mg	1,000 mg	1,000 mg	1,000 mg
Iron	18 mg	18 mg	18 mg	18 mg
Vitamin A	1,000 RE	1,000 RE	1,000 RE	1,000 RE
Vitamin C	60 mg	60 mg	60 mg	60 mg

 * Numbers may be rounded
 ** 46 g is the minimum amount of protein recommended for all calorie levels below 1,800.
 *** 20 g is the minimum amount of fiber recommended for all calorie levels below 2,000.

Note: These calorie levels may not apply to children or adolescents, who have varying calorie requirements. For specific advice concerning calorie levels, please consult a registered dietitian, qualified health professional or pediatrician.

VOLUME MEASUREMENTS (dry)

⅛ teaspoon = 0.5 mL
¼ teaspoon = 1 mL
½ teaspoon = 2 mL
¾ teaspoon = 4 mL
1 teaspoon = 5 mL
1 tablespoon = 15 mL
2 tablespoons = 30 mL
¼ cup = 60 mL
⅓ cup = 75 mL
½ cup = 125 mL
⅔ cup = 150 mL
¾ cup = 175 mL
1 cup = 250 mL
2 cups = 1 pint = 500 mL
3 cups = 750 mL
4 cups = 1 quart = 1 L

VOLUME MEASUREMENTS (fluid)

1 fluid ounce (2 tablespoons) = 30 mL
4 fluid ounces (½ cup) = 125 mL
8 fluid ounces (1 cup) = 250 mL
12 fluid ounces (1½ cups) = 375 mL
16 fluid ounces (2 cups) = 500 mL

WEIGHTS (mass)

½ ounce = 15 g
1 ounce = 30 g
3 ounces = 90 g
4 ounces = 120 g
8 ounces = 225 g
10 ounces = 285 g
12 ounces = 360 g
16 ounces = 1 pound = 450 g

DIMENSIONS

¹⁄₁₆ inch = 2 mm
⅛ inch = 3 mm
¼ inch = 6 mm
½ inch = 1.5 cm
¾ inch = 2 cm
1 inch = 2.5 cm

OVEN TEMPERATURES

250°F = 120°C
275°F = 140°C
300°F = 150°C
325°F = 160°C
350°F = 180°C
375°F = 190°C
400°F = 200°C
425°F = 220°C
450°F = 230°C

BAKING PAN SIZES

Utensil	Size in Inches/Quarts	Metric Volume	Size in Centimeters
Baking or	8×8×2	2 L	20×20×5
Cake Pan	9×9×2	2.5 L	22×22×5
(square or	12×8×2	3 L	30×20×5
rectangular)	13×9×2	3.5 L	33×23×5
Loaf Pan	8×4×3	1.5 L	20×10×7
	9×5×3	2 L	23×13×7
Round Layer	8×1½	1.2 L	20×4
Cake Pan	9×1½	1.5 L	23×4
Pie Plate	8×1¼	750 mL	20×3
	9×1¼	1 L	23×3
Baking Dish	1 quart	1 L	—
or Casserole	1½ quart	1.5 L	—
	2 quart	2 L	—